ATLANTA HAWKS

ALL-TIME GREATS

BY TED COLEMAN

Book design by Jake Slavik
Cover design by Jake Slavik

Photographs ©: Phelan M. Ebenhack/AP Images, cover (top), 1 (top); Al Messerschmidt/AP Images, cover (bottom), 1 (bottom); AP Images, 4, 8; J. M. Hogan/AP Images, 7; William Smith/AP Images, 10; Cliff Welch/Icon Sportswire/AP Images, 13; John Amis/AP Images, 14; Erik S. Lesser/AP Images, 16; Sue Ogrocki/AP Images, 19; Curtis Compton/Atlanta Journal-Constitution/AP Images, 20

Press Box Books, an imprint of Press Room Editions.

ISBN
978-1-63494-599-8 (library bound)
978-1-63494-617-9 (paperback)
978-1-63494-635-3 (epub)
978-1-63494-651-3 (hosted ebook)

Library of Congress Control Number: 2022913236

Distributed by North Star Editions, Inc.
2297 Waters Drive
Mendota Heights, MN 55120
www.northstareditions.com

Printed in the United States of America
Mankato, MN
012023

ABOUT THE AUTHOR

Ted Coleman is a freelance sportswriter and children's book author who lives in Louisville, Kentucky, with his trusty Affenpinscher, Chloe.

TABLE OF CONTENTS

CHAPTER 1

NOMAD HAWKS 4

CHAPTER 2

HIGH FLYERS 10

CHAPTER 3

SEEKING A STAR 16

TIMELINE 22

TEAM FACTS 23

MORE INFORMATION 23

GLOSSARY 24

INDEX 24

PETTIT
9
HAWKS
9
11

CHAPTER 1

NOMAD HAWKS

The Atlanta Hawks moved a lot in their early years. By their seventh season in 1955–56, they were the St. Louis Hawks. Superstar **Bob Pettit** led the Hawks during their most successful era.

Pettit was the second overall draft pick by the Milwaukee Hawks in 1954. The 6'9" Pettit could score like no forward before him. He battled under the hoop to score baskets. That helped him become the first NBA player to score 20,000 career points. Pettit also used his size to pull down lots of rebounds.

STAT SPOTLIGHT

CAREER REBOUNDS

HAWKS TEAM RECORD

Bob Pettit: 12,849

Pettit played with talented teammates. **Cliff Hagan** gave the team an added scoring punch. The forward made five All-Star teams in a row at one point. Pettit and Hagan helped the Hawks make the NBA Finals four times from 1957 to 1961. They played the Boston Celtics each time. The duo averaged 51.9 points per game in the 1958 playoffs. The Hawks won their first championship that year.

Point guard **Lenny Wilkens** helped St. Louis remain a strong team. Wilkens made his debut in 1960. He proved to be a natural fit with Pettit and Hagan. Wilkens had a way of setting up the team's two big scorers.

Pettit retired in 1965. The team's main inside scoring option then was center **Zelmo Beaty**. Beaty was a physical player near the basket. He averaged more than 20 points per game three times for the Hawks.

HUDSON
23

HISTORIC FIRSTS

The Hawks' first home was Moline, Illinois, as the Tri-Cities Blackhawks. In 1946–47, the Blackhawks made history. They had one of the first four Black players in the National Basketball League (NBL) on their team. William "Pop" Gates starred for Tri-City that season. The NBL later joined another league to become the NBA.

Beaty moved with the Hawks to Atlanta in 1968. So did **Bill Bridges**. The forward was just as good a scorer as a rebounder. He averaged 11.9 per game in both statistics over his career.

But Atlanta's biggest star in the early 1970s was swingman **Lou Hudson**. Fans called him "Sweet Lou" for the sweet way he shot. Hudson drove the Hawks offense. He averaged more than 26 points per game in his Hall of Fame career.

ROUNDFIELD
32
bullets

CHAPTER 2
HIGH FLYERS

The first Atlanta teams were high scoring. But Atlanta also played strong defense behind forward **Dan Roundfield**. Fans loved Roundfield for his nonstop effort. He was named to the league's All-Defensive Team five times.

Then there was the man so big they called him tree. **Wayne "Tree" Rollins** stood 7'1". He could easily swat away shots. Opponents found it best to stay away from him.

The Hawks of this era never lacked scoring. **John Drew** was one of the best young scorers in the NBA. He scored 32 points in his NBA debut in 1974. The next season, at 21, he became the youngest All-Star ever. Over eight seasons in Atlanta, Drew averaged more than 21 points per game.

Bob Pettit held every major Hawks record for decades. That began to change when **Dominique Wilkins** arrived in 1982. The "Human Highlight Film" was an incredible athlete. He won two Slam Dunk Contests. But Wilkins could do more than just dunk. He led the NBA with 30.3 points per game in 1985–86.

Supporting Wilkins were players like **Kevin Willis**. The center ranked second only to

STAT SPOTLIGHT

CAREER POINTS

HAWKS TEAM RECORD

Dominique Wilkins: 23,292

WILKINS
21

Pettit in seasons with the Hawks. The 7'1" Willis played in Atlanta for 11 years.

After Wilkins, the Hawks built a new offense led by point guard **Mookie Blaylock**. Blaylock was a skilled passer and three-point shooter. He also could play tough defense. Blaylock led the league in steals in back-to-back years.

Blaylock's backcourt partner in the 1990s was guard **Steve Smith**. Smith was a smooth shooter. He averaged more than 20 points per game in 1996–97 and 1997–98.

On defense, **Dikembe Mutombo** kept opposing players away from the basket. The future Hall of Famer was a master of shot blocking. He won Defensive Player of the Year twice with Atlanta. After swatting away a shot, Mutombo would famously wave his finger to simply say, "No."

TED TURNER

In the late 1970s, the Hawks were possibly going to have to move again. Atlanta businessman Ted Turner put a stop to that. He bought the team in 1977. Turner kept the Hawks in Atlanta for good. He also owned baseball's Braves and was the founder of CNN.

ABDUR-RAHIM

3

CHAPTER 3
SEEKING A STAR

The Hawks struggled to find the next superstar for years. But players like **Jason Terry** kept fans excited. The point guard was quick in his thinking and movements. He was a true scoring threat. He could also make plays for his teammates.

Terry teamed up well with forward **Shareef Abdur-Rahim**. They and **Glenn Robinson** formed the league's highest-scoring trio in 2002–03. Abdur-Rahim could score from anywhere. In November 2001, he recorded one of the Hawks' few 50-point games.

Forward **Josh Smith** was drafted right out of high school. And he arrived with a bang in 2004–05. At 19, he became the second-youngest player to win the Slam Dunk Contest. Smith made an impact on both ends of the court. By the time he left Atlanta he ranked second in Hawks history in blocks and eighth in points.

COACH WILKENS

It took 25 years for Lenny Wilkens to find his way to Atlanta. The former St. Louis Hawk became Atlanta's coach in 1993. Wilkens oversaw some exciting Hawks teams. He led them to the playoffs in all but one of his seven seasons.

Joe Johnson gave the Hawks a new scoring threat. Johnson scored like nobody since Wilkins. He was one of just eight Hawks to average more than 20 points per game. Johnson earned the nickname "Iso Joe" for

ATLANTA
2
JOHNSON
2

his ability to score in one-on-one situations. He also rarely missed a game.

After Johnson, center **Al Horford** became Atlanta's leader. Horford was a skilled two-way player. He helped lead the Hawks to a team-record 60 wins in 2014–15.

The Hawks hoped they had their next superstar in **John Collins**.

The forward nearly doubled his points per game from 10.5 his rookie year to 19.5 the next season.

Collins made that scoring jump playing with rookie point guard **Trae Young** in 2018–19. At only 6'1", there were doubts that Young could succeed in the NBA. He proved those doubts wrong quickly. Young had great court vision. He often set up his teammates to score. He could also score from anywhere on the court. Fans hoped he could be the one to bring a title to Atlanta.

STAT SPOTLIGHT

THREE-POINTERS IN A SEASON

HAWKS TEAM RECORD

Trae Young: 233 (2021–22)

TIMELINE

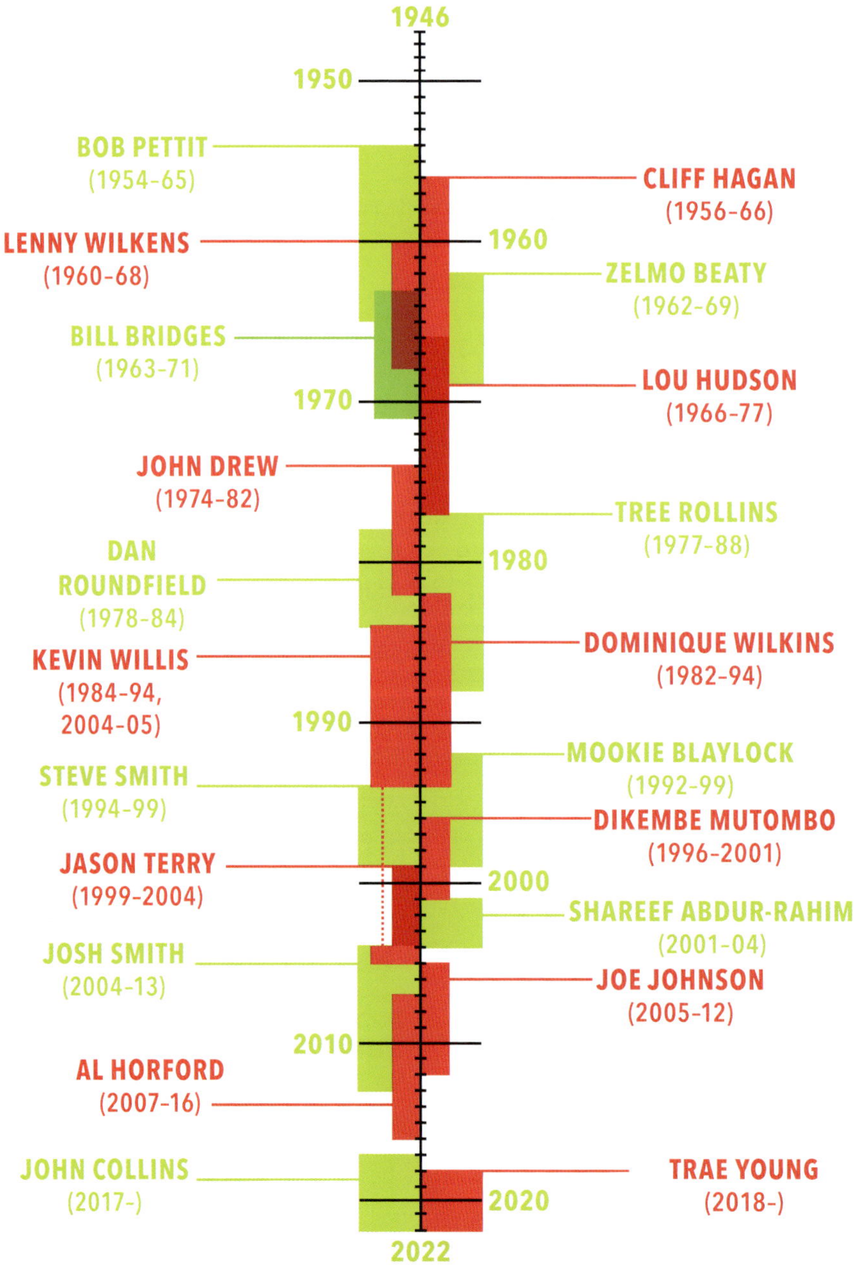
1946
1950
BOB PETTIT
(1954-65)
CLIFF HAGAN
(1956-66)
LENNY WILKENS
(1960-68)
1960
ZELMO BEATY
(1962-69)
BILL BRIDGES
(1963-71)
LOU HUDSON
(1966-77)
1970
JOHN DREW
(1974-82)
TREE ROLLINS
(1977-88)
DAN ROUNDFIELD
(1978-84)
1980
KEVIN WILLIS
(1984-94, 2004-05)
DOMINIQUE WILKINS
(1982-94)
1990
MOOKIE BLAYLOCK
(1992-99)
STEVE SMITH
(1994-99)
DIKEMBE MUTOMBO
(1996-2001)
JASON TERRY
(1999-2004)
2000
SHAREEF ABDUR-RAHIM
(2001-04)
JOSH SMITH
(2004-13)
JOE JOHNSON
(2005-12)
2010
AL HORFORD
(2007-16)
JOHN COLLINS
(2017-)
TRAE YOUNG
(2018-)
2020
2022

TEAM FACTS

ATLANTA HAWKS

Formerly: Buffalo Bisons (1946); Tri-Cities Blackhawks (1946–47 to 1950–51); Milwaukee Hawks (1951–52, 1954–55); St. Louis Hawks (1955–56 to 1967–68)

First season: 1946–47

NBA championships: 1 (1958)*

Key coaches:

Richie Guerin (1964–65 to 1971–72)
327–291, 26–34 playoffs

Lenny Wilkens (1994–95 to 1999–2000)
310–232, 17–30 playoffs

MORE INFORMATION

To learn more about the Atlanta Hawks, go to **pressboxbooks.com/AllAccess**.

These links are routinely monitored and updated to provide the most current information available.

**Through 2021–22 season*

GLOSSARY

debut
First appearance.

draft
A system that allows teams to acquire new players coming into a league.

era
A period of time in history.

highlight
A short video recapping key plays from a game.

retired
Officially ended one's playing career.

rookie
A first-year player.

two-way player
Someone who is skilled at both offensive and defensive play.

INDEX

Abdur-Rahim, Shareef, 17

Beaty, Zelmo, 7, 9
Blaylock, Mookie, 14–15
Bridges, Bill, 9

Collins, John, 20–21

Drew, John, 11–12

Gates, William, 9

Hagan, Cliff, 6–7
Horford, Al, 21
Hudson, Lou, 9

Johnson, Joe, 18, 20

Mutombo, Dikembe, 15

Pettit, Bob, 5–7, 12, 14

Robinson, Glenn, 17
Rollins, Wayne, 11
Roundfield, Dan, 11

Smith, Josh, 18
Smith, Steve, 15

Terry, Jason, 17
Turner, Ted, 15

Wilkens, Lenny, 6–7, 18
Wilkins, Dominique, 12, 14, 18
Willis, Kevin, 12, 14

Young, Trae, 21